on HOPE

POPE FRANCIS

LOYOLA PRESS.
A JESUIT MINISTRY
Chicago

LOYOLA PRESS.
A JESUIT MINISTRY

3441 N. Ashland Avenue
Chicago, Illinois 60657
(800) 621-1008
www.loyolapress.com

Cover art credit: Loyola Press

ISBN: 978-0-8294-4643-2
Library of Congress Control Number: 2017956880

Printed in the United States of America.
17 18 19 20 21 22 Bang 10 9 8 7 6 5 4 3 2 1

Contents

Editor's Note

I have worked as an editor on books by two modern saints and have helped shepherd into print works by some of the most inspiring Catholic writers and teachers of our time. As a cradle Catholic, I have found in these projects many blessings and, always, a closer understanding of my faith and my relationship with Jesus. But there's something about Pope Francis: a quality of mercy, a gentleness of spirit, an intimacy with his faith—it makes me want more of whatever he's got and speaks directly to my heart.

The book you are now holding in your hands is the sixth book Loyola Press, the publishing company I work for, has published by Pope Francis. I mention this because Loyola Press is a Jesuit publisher and Pope Francis is the first Jesuit pope.

But more than being a Jesuit, Pope Francis is the head of the Holy Roman Catholic Church; he is the Vicar of Christ, the spiritual leader of more than 1.2 billion people on the planet, the head of a faith community that is two thousand years old and still going strong—despite what you might see and hear in the secular media.

Pope Francis is the most recognizable person in the world as I'm writing this; he is certainly the most respected religious leader in the world. When the world's most respected religious leader chooses to teach us about something, as Pope Francis has with mercy, it's worthy of our attention.

In this work, Pope Francis has chosen another timely message, this time hope, and specifically Christian hope.

In his opening chapter, Pope Francis writes: "In these times that appear dark, in which we sometimes feel disoriented by the evil and violence that surround us, by the distress of so many of our brothers and sisters, we need hope."

This work is adapted from a series of general audiences Pope Francis presented in Rome from December 2016 through March 2017. Pope Francis offers us a vision of hope that is decidedly different from the prevailing secular view: "Let us keep this in mind: our own assurance will not save us; the only certainty that will save us is that of hope in God."

This small book, then, presents Pope Francis's message of hope to all of us who find ourselves living in difficult situations and difficult times. The hope Pope Francis speaks of is found in the Scriptures, in the pastoral and teaching stories he shares from his own life, in the traditions and teachings of the Church, and always in the loving and transforming heart of our Lord Jesus Christ.

May these words from Pope Francis touch your heart, inspire your soul, and offer you the hope that sustains: "The foundation of Christian hope is what we can be most faithful and certain of—the love that God himself has for each of us."

Joseph Durepos
Chicago, July 2017

We must not let hope abandon us. . . .
Optimism disappoints, but hope does not.
—POPE FRANCIS

CHAPTER ONE

The Comfort of Hope

*T*oday we shall begin a new series of teachings on the theme of *Christian hope*. It is very important, because hope never disappoints. Optimism disappoints, but hope does not. We have such need in these times that can appear dark, in which we sometimes feel disoriented by the evil and violence that surround us, by the distress of so many of our brothers and sisters. We need hope. We feel disoriented and even rather discouraged, because we are powerless and it seems this darkness will never end.

We must not let hope abandon us, because God, with his love, walks with us. "I hope, because God is beside me": we can all say this. Each one of us can say: "I hope, I have hope, because God walks with me." He walks and he holds my hand. God does not leave us to ourselves. The Lord Jesus has conquered evil and has opened the path of life for us.

Let us allow the Lord to teach us what it means to hope. Therefore, let us listen to the words of Sacred Scripture, beginning with the prophet Isaiah, the great messenger of hope.

In the second part of his book, Isaiah addresses the people with his message of comfort: "Comfort, comfort my people, says your God. Speak tenderly to Jerusalem, and cry to her that her warfare is ended, that her iniquity is pardoned. . . . 'A voice cries: In the wilderness prepare the way of the Lord, make straight in the desert a highway for our God. Every valley shall be lifted up, and every mountain and hill be made low; the uneven ground shall become level, and the rough places a plain. And the glory of the Lord shall be revealed, and all flesh shall see

it together, for the mouth of the Lord has spoken'"
(40:1–2, 3–5).

God the Father comforts by raising up comforters,
whom he asks to encourage the people, his children,
by proclaiming that the tribulation has ended,
affliction has ended, and sins have been forgiven.
This is what heals the afflicted and fearful heart. This
is why the prophet Isaiah asks them to prepare the
way of the Lord, to be ready to receive his gifts and
his salvation.

For the people, comfort begins with the opportunity
to walk on God's path, a new path, made straight
and passable, a way prepared in the desert, so as
to make it possible to cross it and return to the
homeland. The prophet addresses the people who are
living the tragedy of the exile in Babylon, and now
they hear that they may return to their land, across
a path made smooth and wide, without valleys and
mountains that make the journey arduous, a level
path across the desert. Thus, preparing that path

means preparing a way of salvation and liberation from every obstacle and hindrance.

The exile was a fraught moment in the history of Israel, when the people had lost everything. The people had lost their homeland, freedom, dignity, and even trust in God. They felt abandoned and hopeless. However, there is the prophet's appeal which reopens the heart to faith. The desert is a place in which it is difficult to live, but precisely there, one can now walk in order to return not only to the homeland, but return to God, and return to hoping and smiling. When we are in darkness, in difficulty, we do not smile, and it is precisely hope which teaches us to smile in order to find the path that leads to God.

One of the first things that can happen to people who distance themselves from God is that they are people who do not smile. Perhaps they can break into a loud laugh, a joke, a chuckle, but their smile is missing. Only hope brings a smile: it is the hopeful smile in the expectation of finding God.

Life is often a desert; it is difficult to walk in life, but if we trust in God it can become beautiful and wide as a highway. Never lose hope, continue to believe, always, in spite of everything. When we are before a child, although we have many problems and many difficulties, a smile comes to us from within, because we see hope in front of us: a child is hope. And in this way, we must be able to discern in life the way of hope which leads us to find God, God who became a child for us. He will make us smile; he will give us everything.

These very words of Isaiah were used by John the Baptist in his preaching that invites us to conversion. This is what he said: "The voice of one crying in the wilderness: Prepare the way of the Lord" (Mt 3:3). It is a voice which cries out where it seems that no one can hear it—for who can listen in the desert?—and which cries out in the disorientation caused by a crisis of faith. We cannot deny that the world today is in a crisis of faith. People say: "I believe in God, I am a Christian." But their lives are far from being

Christian; they are far removed from God. Religion, faith is but an expression: "Do I believe?"—"*Yes!*"

This means returning to God, converting the heart to God and going on this path to find him. He is waiting for us. This is John the Baptist's preaching: Prepare. Prepare for the encounter with this child who will give our smile back to us.

When the Baptist proclaims Jesus' coming, it is as if the Israelites are still in exile, because they are under the Roman dominion, which renders them foreigners in their own homeland, ruled by powerful occupiers who make decisions about their lives.

However, the true history is not the one made by the powerful, but the one made by God together with his little ones. The true history—that which will remain in eternity—is the one that God writes with his little ones: God with Mary, God with Jesus, God with Joseph, God with the little ones. Those little and simple people whom we see around the newborn Jesus: Zechariah and Elizabeth, who were old and barren; Mary, the young virgin maiden betrothed to Joseph; the shepherds, who were scorned and counted for nothing. It is the little ones, made great by their faith, the little ones who are able to continue to hope. Hope is the virtue of the *little ones*. The great ones, those who are satisfied, do not know hope; they do not know what it is.

It is the little ones with God, with Jesus, who transform the desert of exile, of desperation and loneliness, of suffering, into a level plain on which to walk in order to encounter the glory of the Lord.

Let us be confident as we await the coming of the Lord, and what the desert may represent in our life—each one of us knows what desert he or she is walking in—and that it will become a garden in bloom, because hope does not disappoint.

We are called to become men and

women of hope.

—POPE FRANCIS

CHAPTER TWO

Reasons for Hope

Chapter 52 of Isaiah begins with the invitation addressed to Jerusalem to awake, shake off the dust and chains, and put on their most beautiful clothes, because the Lord has come to free his people (vv. 1–3). "My people shall know my name; therefore in that day they shall know that it is I who speak; here am I" (v. 6). It is to this "here am I" said by the Lord, which sums up his firm will for salvation and closeness to us, that Jerusalem responds with a song of joy, according to the prophet's invitation. It is a very important, historic moment. It is the end of the Babylonian exile; it is the opportunity for Israel to rediscover God and, in faith, rediscover itself. The Lord is near, and the small population that survived the exile and whose faith endured [crisis] while in exile, and continued to believe, and to hope even in the midst of darkness—that "remnant" will be able to see the wonders of God.

At this point, the prophet includes a song of exaltation: "How beautiful upon the mountains are the feet of him who brings good tidings, / who proclaims peace, / who proclaims salvation, / who says to Zion, 'Your God reigns' / Break forth together into singing, you waste places of Jerusalem; / for the Lord has comforted his people, / he has redeemed Jerusalem. / The Lord has bared his holy arm before the eyes of all the nations; / and all the ends of the earth shall see the salvation of our God" (Is. 52:7, 9–10).

These words of Isaiah, upon which we want to linger awhile, refer to the miracle of peace, and do so in a very specific way, placing the gaze not on the messenger but on his feet that are running quickly:

"How beautiful upon the mountains are the feet of him who brings good tidings."

He is like the spouse in the Canticle of Canticles who runs toward his beloved: "Behold, he comes, leaping upon the mountains, bounding over the hills" (2:8). Thus, even the messenger of peace runs, bringing the happy announcement of liberation, of salvation, and proclaiming that God reigns.

God has not abandoned his people, and he has not left them to be vanquished by evil, because he is faithful, and his grace is greater than sin. We must learn this, because we are stubborn and do not learn. However, which is greater, God or sin? God is, and which is victorious to the end, God or sin? God, and he is able to defeat the most serious, the most shameful, the most terrible sin, the worst of sins, and with what weapon does God defeat sin? With love! This means that "God reigns" are the words of faith in a Lord whose power bends down to humanity, to offer mercy, and to free man and woman from all that disfigures in them the beautiful image of God, for when we are in sin, God's image is disfigured. The fulfillment of so much love will be the very kingdom instituted by Jesus, that kingdom of forgiveness and peace: the Lord has remitted my sins, the Lord has forgiven me, the Lord has had mercy on me, he came to save me.

These are the reasons for our hope. When everything seems finished, when, faced with many negative realities, and faith becomes demanding, and there comes the temptation which says that nothing makes sense anymore, behold instead the beautiful news brought by those swift feet: God is coming to fulfill something new, to establish a kingdom of peace. God . . . comes to bring freedom and consolation. Evil will not triumph forever; there is an end to suffering. Despair is defeated because God is among us.

And we too are urged to awaken, like Jerusalem, according to the invitation of the prophet; we are called to become men and women of hope, cooperating in the coming of this kingdom made of light and destined for all men and women of hope.

How bad is it when we find a Christian who has lost hope? "But, I don't hope in anything; everything is finished for me," says a Christian who is incapable of looking to the horizons of hope, and before whose heart there is only a wall. However, God destroys such walls with forgiveness. And for this reason, we must pray that each day God may give us hope and give it to everyone, that hope which arises when we see God in the crib in Bethlehem.

The message of the Good News entrusted to us is urgent. We too must run like the messenger on the mountains, because the world cannot wait; humanity is hungry and thirsty for justice, truth, peace. And, seeing the little child of Bethlehem, and the little ones of the world, we will know that the promise was accomplished; the message is fulfilled.

We need to open our hearts to this littleness which is there in that child, and to that great wonder. It is the surprise of a child God, of a poor God, of a weak God, of a God who abandons his greatness to come close to each one of us.

Let us keep this in mind: our own assurance will not save us; the only certainty that will save us is that of hope in God.

—POPE FRANCIS

CHAPTER THREE

Hope Is a Journey

*W*e have begun our journey on the theme of hope. The prophet Isaiah has guided us up to this point. Now, I would like to reflect more specifically on the moment in which hope came into the world, with the incarnation of the Son of God. It was also Isaiah who foretold the birth of the Messiah in several passages: "Behold, a young woman shall conceive and bear a son, and shall call his name Immanuel" (7:14), and also: "There shall come forth a shoot from the stump of Jesse, and a branch shall grow out of his roots" (11:1). In these passages, God fulfills his promise by becoming human; not abandoning his people, he draws near to the point of stripping himself of his divinity. In this way God shows his fidelity and inaugurates a new kingdom, which gives a new hope to mankind. And what is this hope? Eternal life.

When we speak of hope, often it refers to what is not in humanity's power to realize, which is invisible. In fact, what we hope for goes beyond our strength and our perception. But the birth of Christ, inaugurating redemption, speaks to us of a different hope, a dependable, visible, and understandable hope, because it is founded in God. He comes into the world and gives us the strength to walk with him: God walks with us in Jesus, and walking with him toward the fullness of life gives us the strength to dwell in the present in a new way, albeit an arduous one.

For a Christian, to hope means the certainty of being on a journey with Christ toward the Father who awaits us. Hope is never still; hope is always journeying, and it makes us journey. This hope, which the child of Bethlehem gives us, offers a destination, a sure, ongoing goal, salvation of humanity, blessedness to those who trust in a merciful God. Saint Paul summarizes all this with the expression "in this hope we were saved" (Rom. 8:24).

In other words, walking in this world, with hope, we are saved. Here we can each ask ourselves the question, each one of us: Am I walking with hope or is my interior life static, closed? Is my heart a locked drawer or a drawer open to the hope which enables me to walk not alone but with Jesus?

In Christian homes during the Christian season, the Nativity scene is arranged, according to the tradition which dates back to Saint Francis of Assisi. In its simple way, the Nativity scene conveys hope; each one of the characters is immersed in this atmosphere of hope.

First of all, we note the place where Jesus was born: Bethlehem. Bethlehem was a small village in Judea where, hundreds of years earlier, David was born, the shepherd boy chosen by God to be the king of

Israel. Bethlehem is not a capital city and for this reason is preferred by Divine Providence, who loves to act through the little ones and the humble. In that birthplace was born the highly anticipated "Son of David," Jesus, in whom the hope of God and the hope of humanity meet.

We also look to Mary, mother of hope. With her *yes* she opened the door of our world to God: her maiden's heart was full of hope, wholly enlivened by faith; and thus God chose her and she believed in his word. For nine months, Mary was the ark of the new and eternal Covenant, in the grotto, contemplating the child, and seeing in him the love of God, who comes to save his people and the whole of humanity.

Next to Mary is Joseph, a descendant of Jesse and of David; he too believed in the words of the angel, and looking at Jesus in the manger, reflects on the fact that that child has come from the Holy Spirit, and that God himself commanded him to call the child "Jesus." In that name there is hope for every man and woman, because through that son of woman,

God will save humanity from death and from sin. This is why it is important to contemplate the Nativity scene.

In the Nativity scene there are also shepherds, who represent the humble and poor who await the Messiah, the "consolation of Israel" (Lk. 2:25) and the "redemption of Jerusalem" (2:38). In this child they see the realization of the promises and hope that the salvation of God will finally arrive for each of them. Those who trust in their own certainties, especially material, do not await God's salvation.

Let us keep this in mind: our own assurance will not save us; the only certainty that will save us is that of hope in God. It will save us because it is strong and enables us to journey in life with joy, with the will to do good, and to be good, and with the will to attain eternal happiness. The little ones, the shepherds, instead trust in God, hope in him and rejoice when they recognize in that child the sign indicated by the angels.

The very choir of angels proclaims from on high the great design that the child fulfills: "Glory to God in the highest, and on earth peace among men with whom he is pleased" (2:14). Christian hope is expressed in praise and gratitude to God, who has initiated his kingdom of love, justice, and peace.

Every yes we say to Jesus is a seed of hope. Let us trust in this seed of hope, in this yes: "Yes, Jesus, you can save me. You can save me, Lord."

Hope opens new horizons, making us capable of dreaming what is not even imaginable.

—POPE FRANCIS

CHAPTER FOUR

Hoping against Hope

aint Paul, in Romans, reminds us of the great figure of Abraham to show us the way of faith and hope. Of him the apostle writes, "He believed, hoping against all hope, and so became the father of many nations" (Rom. 4:18). "Hoping against hope"—this concept is powerful: even when there is no hope, I hope. This is how our father Abraham hoped. Saint Paul is referring to the faith by which Abraham believed the word of God, who promised him a son. It was truly a hope "against hope," so far-fetched was what the Lord was announcing. Abraham was elderly, almost a hundred years old, and his wife Sarah was barren. But God told Abraham, and he believed.

Trusting in this promise, Abraham set off, agreeing to leave his land and become a stranger in a new land, hoping in this "impossible" son that God would give him, despite the barren womb of Sarah. Abraham believed, and his faith opened him to a hope that appeared unreasonable; such hope is the ability to go beyond human reasoning, wisdom, and prudence of the world, beyond what is normally considered common sense, to believe in the impossible.

Hope opens new horizons, making us capable of dreaming what is not even imaginable. This hope invites us to enter the darkness of an uncertain future and to walk through and into the light. It is beautiful, the virtue of hope; it gives us great strength to walk in life.

But it is a difficult journey, even for Abraham, a crisis of despair. He trusted, he left his home, his land, his friends, everything. He left, went into the land of which God had told him, and the time passed. Traveling was not like today, with planes—arriving at our destination within a few hours. It could take months, years. Time passed, and still the child did not come.

Abraham complained to the Lord. This, too, we learn from our father Abraham: to complain to the Lord is another way of praying. Complain—he is our Father! And this is a way of praying, complaining to the Lord; this is good. Abraham complained to the Lord, saying: "Behold, to me thou hast given no seed, and my servant will be my heir." And behold, came this word from the Lord: "No, that one will not be your heir; your own offspring will be your heir." He took him outside and said: "Look up at the sky and count the stars, if you can. Just so . . . will your descendants be."

The scene takes place at night, and it's dark outside, but also dark in Abraham's heart; there is the darkness of disappointment, discouragement, and difficulty in continuing to hope for something impossible. By now the patriarch is too old, there seems no chance of a son, and it will be a servant who inherits everything.

Abraham still turns to the Lord, but God, even if he is present, does not talk to him; it is as if he had moved away, as if he had not kept his word. And Abraham feels alone, old and tired, death looming. How can he continue to trust?

Nevertheless, Abraham continues to believe in God and hope that something good can still happen. Otherwise, why consult the Lord, why complain to him, why call him back on his promises? For Abraham, hope is not a certainty that keeps us safe from doubt and perplexity. Many times, the hope is dark; but there is still hope, hope that moves you forward. Faith is also struggling with God, showing our bitterness, not accepting "pie-in-the-sky" fictions. But he is the father; he has understood you. You have to have courage, and this is hope. Hope is not being afraid to see reality for what it is and accept the contradictions.

Abraham, in faith, keeps turning to God to help him, to keep him hoping. Curiously, he does not ask for a child. Instead he asks, "Help me to keep hoping"; this is the prayer to have hope. And the Lord insists on keeping his incredible promise that there will be a child, born of Abraham, generated by him. Nothing has changed from God. God continues to repeat what he had said and offers no handholds to Abraham, for him to feel reassured. Abraham's only security is trusting the word of the Lord and continuing to hope.

And that sign that God gives to Abraham is a request to continue to believe and hope: "Look up at the sky and count the stars; so shall your descendants be." It is still a promise; it is still something to look forward to in the future. God takes Abraham outside his tent and shows him the stars. To believe, you must learn to see with the eyes of faith. Yes, they are only stars, everyone can see them, but for Abraham they become a sign of God's faithfulness.

It is this belief, this way of hope, that each of us must travel. Sometimes our only option is to look up at the stars and to trust God. God's hope will not disappoint.

To speak of hope to those who are desperate,
it is essential to share their desperation.
To dry the tears from the faces of those who
are suffering, it is necessary to join our
tears with theirs.

—POPE FRANCIS

CHAPTER FIVE

Tears of Hope

*L*et's reflect on the figure of a woman who speaks to us about hope lived in tears. This is Rachel, wife of Jacob, and mother of Joseph and Benjamin: she who, as the book of Genesis tells us, dies while giving birth to her second-born son, who is Benjamin.

The prophet Jeremiah refers to Rachel as he addresses the Israelites in exile, trying to console them with words full of emotion and poetry; that is, he takes up Rachel's lament, but offers hope: "Thus says the Lord: 'A voice is heard in Ramah, / lamentation and bitter weeping. / Rachel is weeping for her children; / she refuses to be comforted for her children, / because they are not.'"

In these verses, Jeremiah presents a woman of his people, the great matriarch of the tribe, in a situation of suffering and tears but along with an unexpected outlook on life. Rachel, who in the Genesis account had died in childbirth and had accepted that death so that her son might live, is now instead represented by the prophet as alive in Ramah, where the deportees have gathered, weeping for the children who in a certain sense died going into exile; children who, as she herself says, "are no more"; they are lost forever.

For this reason Rachel does not want to be consoled. This refusal of hers expresses the depth of her pain and the bitterness of her tears. In the face of the tragedy of the loss of her children, a mother cannot accept words or gestures of consolation, which are always inadequate, never capable of alleviating the pain of a wound that cannot and does not want to be healed, a pain proportionate to her love.

Every mother knows this; and there are many mothers who weep, who do not accept the loss of a child, inconsolable before a death that is impossible to accept. Rachel holds within her the pain of all the mothers of the world, of all time, and the tears of every human being who suffers irreparable loss.

This refusal of Rachel, who does not want to be consoled, also teaches us how much sensitivity is asked of us before other people's suffering. In order to speak of hope to those who are desperate, it is essential to share their desperation. In order to dry the tears from the faces of those who are suffering, it is necessary to join our tears with theirs. Only in this way are our words capable of giving a little hope. If I cannot speak words in this way, with tears, with suffering, then silence is better: a caress, a gesture, but no words.

God, with his sensitivity and his love, responds to Rachel's tears with true words, not contrived. Jeremiah's text continues in this way: "Thus says the Lord"—he responds to those tears—"'Keep your voice from weeping, and your eyes from tears; / for your work shall be rewarded, says the Lord, / and they shall come back from the land of the enemy. / There is hope for your future, says the Lord, / and your children shall come back to their own country'" (Jer. 31:16–17).

Precisely through the mother's tears, there is still hope for the children, who will return to life. This woman, who had accepted death at the moment of childbirth so that the child might live, becomes with her tears the beginning of new life for the children who are exiled far from their homeland. To the suffering and bitter tears of Rachel, the Lord responds with a promise that can now be the source of true consolation for her: the people will be able to return from exile and freely experience in faith their own relationship with God. The tears generate hope. This is not easy to understand, but it is true. So often in our life, tears sow hope; they are the seeds of hope.

As we know, this text of Jeremiah is later taken up by the evangelist Matthew and applied to the massacre of the innocents (see Matt. 2:16–18). This text places before us the tragedy of the killing of defenseless human beings, the horror of a power that scorns and terminates life. The children of Bethlehem die because of Jesus. And he, the innocent Lamb, then dies in turn, for all of us. The Son of God entered the suffering of mankind. This must not be forgotten.

When someone asks me a difficult question, like "Tell me, Father: why do children suffer?" truly, I do not know how to respond. I say only: "Look at the Crucifix: God gave us his Son, he suffered, and perhaps you will find an answer there." But there are no easy answers. Just looking at the love of God, who gives his Son, who offers his life for us, can indicate a path of consolation. For this reason, we say that the Son of God entered the pain of mankind; he shared it, and embraced death; his Word is definitively the word of consolation, because it is born of suffering.

On the Cross, it will be he, the dying Son, entrusting to his mother the disciple John, and making her mother of the people of faith. Death is conquered, and thus Jeremiah's prophecy is fulfilled. Mary's tears, too, like those of Rachel, generate hope and new life.

Here is the wonderful reality of hope:
in trusting in the Lord, we become like him.
His blessing transforms us into his children
who share in his life.
—POPE FRANCIS

CHAPTER SIX

The Reality of Hope

ope is a basic human need: hope for the future, a belief in life, and so-called positive thinking.

But it is important that this hope be placed in what can really help us live and can give meaning to our existence. This is why Scripture warns us against the false hopes that the world presents to us, exposing their uselessness and demonstrating their foolishness. It does so in various ways, but especially by denouncing the falsehood of the idols in which humanity is continually tempted to place our trust, making them the object of our hope.

The prophets and scholars insist on [denouncing idols], touching a nerve of the believer's journey of faith. Faith means trusting in God—those who have faith trust in God—but there's a moment when, in meeting life's difficulties, we can experience the fragility of that trust and feel the need for various certainties, for tangible, concrete assurances. I entrust myself to God, but there is a situation that is rather serious and I need a little more concrete reassurance. And there lies the danger.

We are tempted to seek ephemeral consolations that seem to fill the void of loneliness and alleviate the fatigue of believing. We think we can find them in the security that money can give, in alliances with the powerful, in worldliness, in false ideologies. Sometimes we look for them in a god that can bend to our requests and magically intervene to change the situation and make it as we wish, an idol, indeed, that in itself can do nothing. It is impotent and deceptive. But we like idols; we love them, in fact.

Once, in Buenos Aires, I had to go from one church to another, a thousand meters, more or less. I did so on foot, and between them there was a park, and in the park there were little tables, where many, many fortune-tellers were sitting. It was full of people who were waiting in line. You gave them your hand and they would begin, but the conversation was always the same: "There is a woman in your life, there is a darkness coming, but not to worry, everything will be fine." Then, you paid. This gives us security?! It is the security of—allow me to use the word—nonsense. When you go to a seer or to a fortune-teller who reads cards, this is an idol, and when we are attached to them, we buy false hope. Whereas, in the gratuitous hope, that Jesus Christ brought us freely, giving his life for us, sometimes we fail to fully trust.

A psalm brimming with wisdom depicts in a very suggestive way the falsity of these idols that the world offers for our hope and on which men and women of all ages are tempted to rely. It is Psalm 115, which is recited as follows: "Their idols are silver and gold,

/ the work of men's hands. / They have mouths, but do not speak; / eyes, but do not see. / They have ears, but do not hear; / noses, but do not smell. / They have hands, but do not feel; / feet, but do not walk; / and they do not make a sound in their throat. / Those who make them are like them; / so are all who trust in them!" (4–8).

The psalmist also presents to us, a bit ironically, the absolutely ephemeral character of these idols. And we must understand that these are not merely figures made of metal or other materials, but they are also those we build in our minds: when we trust in limited realities that we transform into absolute values, or when we diminish God to fit our own template and our own ideas of divinity.

A god who looks like us is understandable, predictable, just like the idols mentioned in the psalm. Man, the image of God, manufactures a god in his own image, but it is a poorly realized image. It does not hear, does not act, and above all, it cannot speak. But we are happier to turn to idols than to turn to the Lord. Many times we are happier with the ephemeral hope that a false idol gives us than with the great and sure hope that the Lord gives us.

In contrast to hoping in a Lord of life who through his Word created the world and leads our existence, we turn to silent effigies—including ideologies with their claim to the absolute; like wealth, this is a great idol. Also, power and success, vanity, with their illusion of eternity and omnipotence, values such as physical beauty and health. When they become idols to which everything is sacrificed, they become things that confuse the mind and the heart, and instead of supporting life, they lead to death. It is terrible to hear, and painful to the soul, something that once, years ago, I heard in the diocese of Buenos Aires: a good woman—very beautiful—boasted about her beauty. She said, as if it were natural, "Yes, I had to have an abortion because my figure is very important." These are idols, and they lead you down the wrong path, and do not give you happiness.

The message of the psalm is very clear: if you place hope in idols, you become like them: hollow images with hands that do not feel, feet that do not walk, mouths that cannot speak. You no longer have anything to say; you become unable to help, to change things, unable to smile, to give of yourself, incapable of love. We need to abide in the world but defend ourselves from the world's illusions.

As the psalm continues, we must trust and hope in God, and God will bestow the blessing. So says the Psalm: "O Israel, trust in the Lord. . . . O House of Aaron, put your trust in the Lord. . . . You who fear the Lord, trust in the Lord. . . . The Lord has been mindful of us; he will bless us" (Ps. 115:9, 10, 11, 12).

The Lord always remembers. Even in the bad times he remembers, and this is our hope. And his hope does not disappoint: never, never. Idols always disappoint; they are make-believe; they are not real. Here is the wonderful reality of hope: in trusting in the Lord, we become like him. His blessing transforms us into his children who share in his life.

Hope in God allows us to enter within the range of his remembrance, of his memory that blesses us and saves us. It is then that a hallelujah can burst forth in praise to the living and true God, who was born for us of Mary, died on the Cross, and rose again in glory. In this God we have hope, and it is this God—who is not an idol—who never disappoints.

Prayer leads us forward in hope.

—POPE FRANCIS

CHAPTER SEVEN

Prayer and Hope

*I*n Sacred Scripture, among the prophets of Israel, a rather anomalous figure stands out, a prophet who attempts to avoid the Lord's call by refusing to place himself at the service of the divine plan of salvation. It is the prophet Jonah, whose story is narrated in a small book of only four chapters, a type of parable that bears a great lesson, that of the mercy of God who forgives.

Jonah is a prophet "going out" and also a prophet in flight. He is an "outgoing" prophet whom God sends "to the periphery," to Nineveh, in order to convert the people of that great city. But Nineveh, to an Israelite like Jonah, is a threatening reality, the enemy that places Jerusalem itself in peril, and therefore is to be destroyed, certainly not to be saved. Therefore, when God sends Jonah to preach in that city, the prophet, who knows the Lord's goodness and his desire to forgive, seeks to avoid his task and flees.

During his flight, the prophet enters contact with pagans, the mariners on the ship he boarded to distance himself from God and his mission. He flees far away (Nineveh was in the area we now know as Iraq), and he flees all the way to Spain. And it is actually the behavior of these pagan men, as that of the people of Nineveh later on, that today allows us to reflect a bit on the hope which, in the face of danger and death, is expressed in prayer.

Indeed, during the sea voyage, a mighty storm breaks out, and Jonah goes down to the ship's cargo hold and falls asleep. The mariners, however, seeing themselves lost, "each cried to his god." The captain of the ship wakes Jonah, saying to him, "What do you mean, you sleeper? Arise, call upon your god!

Perhaps your god will give a thought to us, that we do not perish" (Jon. 1:6).

The reaction of these "pagans" is the right reaction in the face of death, in the face of danger, because it is then that man fully experiences his frailty and his need for salvation.

The instinctive dread of dying reveals the necessity of hope in the God of life. "Perhaps God will give a thought to us that we do not perish" are the words of hope that become prayer, that supplication filled with anguish that rises to our lips in the face of an imminent danger of death.

We too easily disdain turning to God in need as if it were only a prayer of self-interest and therefore imperfect. But God knows our weakness. He knows that we remember him in order to ask for help, and with the indulging smile of a father, God responds benevolently.

When Jonah, recognizing his responsibility, throws himself into the sea to save his travel companions, the storm quiets down. Certain death leads these pagan men to prayer, enabling the prophet, in spite of it all, to live his vocation in service to others, sacrificing himself for them. And now he leads the survivors to recognize and praise the true Lord. The mariners who, in the grip of fear, have prayed to their gods, now, with sincere fear of the Lord, recognize the true God, offer sacrifices, and make vows. Hope, which has induced them to pray to be spared from death, is revealed as even more powerful and ushers in a reality that goes beyond what they were hoping: not only do they not perish in the storm, but they also become open to recognizing the one true Lord of heaven and earth.

Afterward, even the people of Nineveh, with the prospect of being destroyed, pray, spurred by hope in God's forgiveness. They do penance, invoke the Lord, and convert to him, beginning with the king who, like the ship's captain, gives voice to hope: "Who knows? God may yet repent and turn from his fierce anger, so that we perish not" (Jon. 3:9).

For them, too, as for the crew in the storm, facing death and being saved from it leads them to the truth. Thus, under divine mercy, and even more in the light of the Paschal Mystery, death can become, as it was for Saint Francis of Assisi, "our sister death" and represent, for every person, for each one of us, the surprising occasion to know hope and encounter the Lord.

May the Lord help us to understand this link between prayer and hope. Prayer leads us forward in hope, and when things become dark, more prayer is needed, and there we will find even more hope.

Let us never set conditions for God;
let us instead allow hope to conquer our fears.

—POPE FRANCIS

CHAPTER EIGHT

The Language of Hope

*A*mong the figures of women presented to us by the Old Testament, one great heroine stands out among the people: Judith. The biblical book which bears her name recounts the massive military campaign of King Nebuchadnezzar, who ruled over Nineveh. He expanded the boundaries of his empire by defeating and enslaving all the surrounding people. The reader senses what it is like to face a great, invincible enemy who is spreading death and destruction. When King Nebuchadnezzar reaches the Promised Land, he places the lives of all Israel's children in jeopardy.

Indeed, Nebuchadnezzar's army, under the leadership of General Holofernes, lays siege to the Judean city of Bethulia, cutting off the water supply and wearing down the people's resistance.

The situation is dramatic, to the point that the city's inhabitants turn to the elders, demanding that they surrender to the enemy. Their words are desperate: "For now we have no one to help us; God has sold us into their hands, to strew us on the ground before them with thirst and utter destruction." They have reached the point of saying, "God has sold us," their desperation is so great. "Now call them in and surrender the whole city to the army of Holofernes and to all his forces, to be plundered" (Jdt. 7:25–26). The end seems inevitable, the ability to trust in God exhausted. How often have we reached the limit of a situation, where we do not feel able to have faith in the Lord? Paradoxically, it seems to the people that, to escape death, there's nothing left but to surrender into the hands of those who are killers. They know that these soldiers have come to loot the city, to take the women as slaves, and then kill everyone else. This really is "the limit."

Faced with so much despair, the leader of the people attempts to offer some hope: resist for five more days, waiting for God's salvific intervention. However, it is a weak hope which makes him decide: "But if these days pass by, and no help comes for us, I will do what you say" (Jdt. 7:31). Poor man: he has no way out. God is given five days—and here is the sin—God is given five days to intervene, five days of waiting, but already with the prospect of the end. They give God five days to save them, but they know they do not have faith and are expecting the worst. In fact, there is no one among the people still capable of hope. They are desperate.

It is in this situation that Judith appears on the scene. A widow, a woman of great beauty and wisdom, she speaks to the people with the language of faith. Courageously, she reproaches the people to their faces: "You are putting the Lord Almighty to the test. . . . No, my brethren, do not provoke the Lord our God to anger. For if he does not choose to help us within these five days, he has power to protect us within any time he pleases, or even to destroy us in the presence of our enemies. . . . Therefore, while we wait for his deliverance, let us call upon him to help us, and he will hear our voice, if it pleases him" (Jdt. 8:13, 14–15, 17). It is the language of hope. Let us knock on the doors to God's heart. He is the Father; he can save us. This woman, a widow, risks making a fool of herself in front of others. But she is courageous. She goes forward. Now, this is my opinion, but women are more courageous than men.

And with the strength of a prophet, Judith rebukes the men of her people to restore their faith in God; with the gaze of a prophet, she sees beyond the narrow horizon proposed by the leaders, which fear limits even further. God will surely act, she says, while the proposal of waiting five days is a way to tempt him and escape his will. The Lord is the God of salvation—and she believed this—whatever form it may take. It is salvation to liberate from enemies and to bring life, but, in his impenetrable plans, it can also be salvation to allow death. A woman of faith, she knows this. Thus, we know the end, how the story ends: God saves.

But let us never set conditions for God, and let us instead allow hope to conquer our fears. Entrusting ourselves to God means entering his plans without demanding anything, and also accepting that his salvation and his help come to us in ways that differ from our expectations. We ask the Lord for life, for health, for love, for happiness, and it is right to do so, but with the understanding that God is able to bring life even from death, that we can experience peace even in sickness, and that there can be calm even in loneliness, and happiness even in tears. It is not for us to instruct God about what he must do, about what we need. He knows better than we do, and we must have faith, because his ways and his thoughts are different from ours.

The path which Judith shows us is one of faith, of waiting peacefully, of prayer, and of obedience. It is the path of hope. Doing everything within our power, but always remaining in the furrow of the Lord's will. Judith prayed, spoke to the people, and then, courageously, she went, and looked for a way to get close to the leader of the enemy army. Somehow she managed to cut off his head, to slit his throat. She was courageous in her faith and in her deeds. And she always sought out the Lord. Judith, in fact, had her own plan, carried it out successfully, and led her people to victory. But always with the attitude of faith of those who accept everything from the hand of God, certain of his goodness.

Thus Judith, a woman full of faith and courage, restored strength to her people, who were in mortal danger, and guided them along the paths of hope, also pointing them out to us. If we reflect a little, how often have we heard the wise, courageous words of humble people, of humble women? They speak the words of God's wisdom. How often do grandmothers know the right thing to say, the word of hope, because they have life experience? They have suffered greatly, and yet they have entrusted themselves to God, and the Lord gives them the gift of encouraging others to hope. And going along those paths, there will be Paschal joy and light in entrusting oneself to the Lord with Jesus' words: "Father, if thou art willing, remove this cup from me; nevertheless, not my will, but thine, be done" (Lk. 22:42). This, then, is the prayer of wisdom, of faith, and of hope.

Christian hope is having the certainty that I am walking toward something that is, not something that I hope may be.

—POPE FRANCIS

CHAPTER NINE

Christian Hope Is the Expectation of Something Already Fulfilled

*W*e have been exploring the theme of hope from the pages of the Old Testament. Now, let's move on to shed light on the extraordinary importance this virtue assumed in the New Testament, represented by the fresh hope of Jesus Christ in the Paschal event. Remember, we Christians are men and women of hope.

It is what clearly emerges in the first letter of Saint Paul to the Thessalonians. One can perceive all the freshness and beauty of the first Christian proclamation. Thessalonica is a young community, quite recently founded; yet, despite its difficulties and many trials, it is rooted in the faith and celebrates with enthusiasm and joy the Resurrection of the Lord Jesus. So the apostle congratulates everyone warmly, as, reborn in the Paschal Mystery, they become truly "sons of light and sons of the day" (1 Thes. 5:5), by virtue of their full communion with Christ.

When Paul writes to them, the community of Thessalonica, only a few years separate his letter from Christ's Easter event. The apostle tries to make everyone understand the effects and consequences of this unique and decisive event: the Resurrection of the Lord and what it signifies for history and in the life of each one. In particular, the community had difficulty not so much in recognizing the Resurrection of Jesus (everyone believed it) but in believing in the resurrection of the dead. Yes, Jesus is risen, but the difficulty was in believing that the dead would rise. In this sense, Paul's letter is more relevant than ever.

Each time we face our own death, or that of a person who is dear, we feel that our faith is put to the test. All our doubts emerge, all our frailty, and we ask ourselves: "But will there truly be life after death? Will I still be able to see and embrace again the people I have loved?" A woman asked me this question several days ago: "Will I meet my loved ones?" In the current context, we need to return to the root and foundation of our faith, to become aware of how much God did for us in Jesus Christ and what our death means. We all are afraid because of this uncertainty about death. It reminds me of an elderly man who said: "I am not afraid of death. But I am a bit afraid seeing it approaching."

Paul, before the fears and perplexity of the community, urges it to wear hope firmly on the head like a helmet, "the hope of salvation," especially in the trials and most difficult times of life. Hope is a helmet. This is what Christian hope is.

When we speak about hope, we can be led to interpret it according to the common meaning of the term *hope*—that is, a reference to something beautiful that we desire but that may or may not be attained. We "hope" something will happen; this is a desire. People say, for example, "I hope there will be good weather tomorrow," but we know that there might be bad weather the following day. Christian hope is not like this. Christian hope is the expectation of something that has already been fulfilled; the door is there, and I hope to reach the door. What do I have to do? Walk toward the door. I am certain that I will reach the door.

This is what Christian hope is: having the certainty that I am walking toward something that *is*, not something that I hope may be. This is Christian hope. Christian hope is the expectation of something that has already been fulfilled and that will certainly be fulfilled for each one of us. Our resurrection too, and that of our departed loved ones, therefore, is not something that may or may not happen but is a certain reality, because it is rooted in the event of Christ's Resurrection. Thus, to hope means to learn how to live in expectation. To learn how to live in expectation and find life.

When a woman realizes she is pregnant, every day she learns to live in the expectation of seeing the gaze of her child that is to come. In this way, too, we must live and learn from these human expectations and live in the expectation of seeing the Lord, of encountering the Lord. This is not easy, but we can learn: to live in expectation. To hope means and entails a humble heart, a poor heart. Only the poor know how to wait. Those who are already full of themselves and of their achievements are not able to place their trust in anyone other than themselves.

Saint Paul writes: "Jesus Christ, who died for us so that whether we wake or sleep we might live with him" (1 Thes. 5:10). These words always generate great comfort and peace for me. We are also called to pray for the beloved people who have left us, that they may live in Christ and be in full communion with us. Something that touches my heart deeply is an expression of Saint Paul, also addressed to the

Thessalonians. It fills me with certain hope when he says, "And so we shall always be with the Lord" (4:17). This is wonderful: everything passes, but after death, we shall always be with the Lord. It is the total certainty of hope, the same which, long before, made Job exclaim: "I know that my Redeemer lives . . . whom I shall see on my side, and my eyes shall behold" (Job 19:25, 27). And so we shall always be with the Lord. Do you believe this? I am asking you: do you believe this?

To feel stronger, I invite you to say it with me three times: "And so, we shall always be with the Lord." And there, with the Lord, we will meet. Thus, let us ask the Lord to teach our hearts to hope in the resurrection; this way we can learn to live in the certain expectation of the encounter with him and with all our loved ones.

No one learns to hope alone.

—POPE FRANCIS

CHAPTER TEN

The Holy Spirit Is the Living Sign of God's Hope

*S*aint Paul, in the first letter to the Thessalonians, exhorts the faithful to remain deeply rooted in the hope of resurrection with that beautiful phrase: "We shall always be with the Lord" (4:17). In the same context, the apostle shows that Christian hope has not only a personal, individual scope, but a communitarian, ecclesial one. We all hope; we all have hope; also as a community we have hope.

For this reason, the gaze is immediately broadened by Paul to all the situations that make up the

Christian community, asking them to pray for one another and to support one another. That we help one another. But not only that we help one another in the many needs of daily life—that we help one another hope, support one another in hope. It is not a coincidence that we begin precisely by referring to those who are entrusted with responsibility and pastoral guidance. They are the first to be called to nourish hope, and this is not because they are better than the others but by virtue of a divine ministry that goes far beyond their strength. For this reason, they need, more than ever, everyone's respect, understanding, and benevolent support.

Attention is then placed on the brothers and sisters most at risk of losing hope, of succumbing to despair. We always hear news of people who succumb to despair and do bad things. Despair leads them to many bad things; we are speaking of the one who is discouraged, one who is weak, one who feels discouraged by the burden of life and of one's own faults, and one who no longer manages to pick him- or herself up.

In these cases, the closeness and warmth of the entire Church must be even more intense and loving, and must take on the exquisite form of compassion, which is not simply sympathy. Compassion is to endure with the other, to suffer with the other, to draw near to the one who is suffering. A word, a caress, but given from the heart; this is compassion, for the one who needs comfort and consolation. This is more important than ever. Christian hope cannot do without genuine and concrete charity. The apostle to the Gentiles himself, in the letter to the Romans, affirms with his heart in his hand: "We who are strong"—for we who have faith, hope, or do not have many difficulties—"ought to bear with the failings of the weak, and not to please ourselves" (15:1). To bear with the weaknesses of others, this witness, then, does not remain closed within the confines of the Christian community. Instead, it echoes in all its vigor beyond it, into the social and civil context, as an appeal not to build walls but bridges, not to exchange evil for evil but to conquer evil with good, offense with forgiveness—a Christian must never say, "You will pay for this!" Never; this is not a Christian gesture; offense is defeated by forgiveness—to live in peace with everyone. This is the Church, and this is what motivates Christian hope, when it takes a strong line while maintaining love at the same time. Love is strong and tender. It is beautiful.

We understand that we do not learn to hope alone. No one learns to hope alone. It is impossible. Hope, to be nourished, necessarily needs a "body" in which the various members support and revive each other. This means, then, that if we hope, it is because many of our brothers and sisters have taught us to hope and have kept our hope alive. Distinguishable among these are the little ones, the poor, the simple, and the marginalized. Because one who is enclosed within his own well-being does not know hope: he hopes only in his well-being and this is not hope: it is relative security; one who is enclosed in his own fulfillment, who always feels that all is well, does not know hope.

Instead, those who hope are those who each day experience trials, precariousness, and their own limitations. These brothers and sisters give us the strongest, most beautiful witness, because they stand firm, trusting in the Lord, knowing that, beyond the sadness, oppression, and inevitability of death, the last word will be his, and it will be a word of mercy, of life, and of peace. Whoever hopes, hopes to one day hear this word: "Come, come to me, brother; come, come to me, sister, for all eternity."

The natural dwelling of our hope is a supportive "body"; for Christian hope this body is the Church, while the vital breath, the soul of this hope, is the Holy Spirit. Without the Holy Spirit one cannot have hope. This is why the apostle Paul invites us to continuously invoke the Spirit to the end. If it is not easy to believe, and it is far less easy to hope, then it is more difficult to hope than to believe. But when the Holy Spirit abides in our hearts, it is he who makes us understand that we must not fear, that the Lord is near, and takes care of us; and it is the Holy Spirit who forms our communities, in a perennial Pentecost, as a living sign of hope for the whole human family.

The foundation of Christian hope is what we can be most faithful and certain of . . . the love that God himself has for each of us.

—POPE FRANCIS

CHAPTER ELEVEN

Christian Hope Is Steadfast

From the time we are small, we are taught that it is not nice to boast. Boasting about what one is or what one has, apart from a certain arrogance, also reveals a lack of respect toward others, especially toward those who are less fortunate. In the apostle Paul's letter to the Romans, however, Paul surprises us at least twice when he exhorts us to boast. Of what, then, is it right to boast? Because if he exhorts us to boast, then it is right to boast about something. And how is it possible to do this without offending others, without excluding someone?

In the first case, we are invited to boast of the abundance of the grace with which we are permeated, in Jesus Christ, by way of the faith. Paul wants to make us understand that, if we learn to read everything in the light of the Holy Spirit, we realize that everything is grace. Everything is a gift. If we pay attention, in fact—in history, as in our life—it is not only we who are acting but above all it is God. He is the absolute protagonist who creates everything as a gift of love, who weaves his plan of salvation, and who leads it to fulfillment for us, through his Son Jesus.

We are asked to recognize all this, to welcome it with gratitude and to make it become a source of praise, of blessing, and of great joy. If we do this, we are at peace with God and we experience freedom. This peace is then extended to all the areas and to all the relationships of our life: we are at peace with ourselves, we are at peace in our family, in our community, at work, and with the people we encounter each day on our journey.

Paul, however, exhorts us to boast even in tribulation. This is not easy to understand. This is more difficult for us and it may seem to have nothing to do with the condition of peace just described. However, it constitutes its truest, most authentic premise.

Indeed, the peace the Lord offers us and guarantees us is not to be understood as the absence of worry, of disappointment, of failure, of reasons for suffering. If it were so, supposing we had managed to be at peace, that moment would end quickly, and we would inevitably fall prey to unease. The peace that springs from faith is a gift: it is the grace of feeling that God loves us and that he is always beside us; he does not leave us on our own even for a moment of our life. This, as the apostle states, generates patience, because we know that, even at the hardest and most disturbing moment, the Lord's mercy and goodness are greater than everything, and nothing will tear us from his hands and from communion with him.

Here, then, is why Christian hope is steadfast; here is why it does not disappoint. Never does it disappoint. Hope does not disappoint. It is not based on what we can do or be, or even on what we may believe in. The foundation of Christian hope is what we can be most faithful and certain of, that is to say, the love that God himself has for each of us. It is easy to say, "God loves us." We all say it. But think a bit: each one of us is able to ask, "Am I sure that God loves me?" It is not so easy to say it. But it is true. This is a good exercise, to say to oneself, "God loves me." This is the root of our certainty, the root of hope.

The Lord has abundantly poured into our hearts the Spirit—who is the love of God—as artisan, as guarantor, precisely so that he may nourish the faith within us and keep this hope alive. This is a certainty: God loves me. "But in this difficult moment?"—God loves me. "I, who have done this bad and cruel thing?"—God loves me. No one can take this certainty away. We must repeat it as a prayer: God loves me. I am sure that God loves me. I am sure that God loves me.

Now we can understand why the apostle Paul exhorts us to always boast about all this. I boast of God's love because he loves me. The hope that we have been given never divides us from others; much less does it lead us to discredit or marginalize them. Instead it is an extraordinary gift of which we are called to make ourselves "channels," with humility and simplicity, for everyone. So our boastfulness is because we have as Father a God who is impartial, who does not exclude anyone, but who opens his house to all human beings, beginning with the least and the most distant, so that as his children we may learn to console and support one another. And never forget: hope does not disappoint.

We have been saved by the Lord
and have begun to contemplate,
in ourselves and in what surrounds us,
the signs of the Resurrection, of Easter,
which brings about the new Creation.
This is the content of our hope.
—POPE FRANCIS

CHAPTER TWELVE

The Breath of Our Hope

*P*eople are often tempted to think that creation is our property, a possession that we can exploit as we please and for which we must account to no one. In his letter to the Romans, the apostle Paul reminds us that, instead, creation is a wondrous gift that God has placed in our hands so that we may enter a relationship with him and may recognize in it the imprint of his loving plan, the fulfillment of which calls us all to work together, day after day.

However, when we human beings allow ourselves to succumb to selfishness, we can end up defacing even the most beautiful things that we have been entrusted to care for. This has happened with creation. Let us think about water. Water is something beautiful and very important. Water gives us life; it helps us in everything, but, to exploit minerals, water is contaminated: creation is sullied, creation is destroyed. This is just one example. There are many others. With the tragic experience of sin, our broken communion with God, we have shattered the original communion with all that surrounds us and we have ended by corrupting creation, thereby rendering it a slave, subjugated to our shortsightedness.

Unfortunately, the result of all this is dramatically before our eyes, every day. When communion with God is broken, humanity loses its original beauty and ends up disfiguring everything around it; all is now marked by the sad, desolate signs of pride and human greed. Human pride, in exploiting creation, destroys.

The Lord, however, does not leave us on our own, and even in this distressing context, he offers us a new prospect of freedom, of universal salvation. It is what Paul highlights joyfully, inviting us to listen to the groans of the whole of creation. Indeed, if we pay attention, around us everything is groaning: Creation itself groans; we human beings groan and the Holy Spirit groans within us, in our hearts.

Now, these groans are not a barren, disconsolate lament, but—as the apostle explains—they are the groaning of a woman in labor; they are the groans of those who suffer but know that a new life is about to be born. And in our case, it is truly so. We are still gripped by the consequences of our sin. Everything around us still bears the signs of our weariness, of our shortcomings, of our closure. At the same time, however, we know that we have been saved by the Lord and that we have already been able to contemplate and to have a foretaste of, in ourselves and in what surrounds us, the signs of the Resurrection, of Easter, which brings about the new Creation.

This is the content of our hope. The Christian does not live outside of the world; she knows how to recognize, in her life and in what surrounds her, the signs of evil, of selfishness, and of sin. She is in solidarity with those who suffer, with those who weep, with those who are marginalized, with those who despair. At the same time, the Christian has learned to read all of this with the eyes of Easter, with the eyes of the risen Christ. Thus, she knows that we are living in the time of waiting, the time of longing which transcends the present, a time of fulfillment.

In hope we know that the Lord wants to definitively heal with his mercy the wounded and humiliated hearts, and all that humans have spoiled by our impiety, and that in this way, God regenerates a new world and a new humanity, finally reconciling them in his love.

How often are we Christians tempted to give in to disappointment, to pessimism? At times, we allow ourselves to resort to pointless complaining, or we remain speechless and do not even know what to ask for, what to hope. Yet once more, the Holy Spirit—the breath of our hope, who keeps the groans and the expectation alive in our heart—comes to help us. The Spirit sees for us beyond the negative semblance of the present and reveals to us the new heavens and the new earth that the Lord is preparing for us all.

Lent is the sacramental sign of our journey from slavery to freedom, always to be renewed. It is certainly a demanding journey, as it rightly should be, because love is demanding, but it is a journey filled with hope.

—POPE FRANCIS

CHAPTER THIRTEEN

Lent, a Time of Hope

O n Ash Wednesday, we enter the liturgical season of Lent. I would like to suggest Lent to you as your personal journey of hope.

Indeed, this prospect is immediately evident if we consider that Lent was instituted in the Church as a time of preparation for Easter and that, therefore, the whole meaning of this forty-day period is illuminated by the Paschal Mystery toward which it is directed. We can imagine the risen Lord who calls us to come out of our darkness, and so we set ourselves on the path toward the One who is Light. Lent is a journey toward the risen Jesus; it is a period of repentance, also of mortification, not as an end but rather aimed at enabling us to rise with Christ, to renew our baptismal identity, that is, to be born anew "of the Spirit," by the love of God. This is why Lent is, by nature, a time of hope.

In order to better understand what this means, we must refer to the fundamental experience of the exodus of the Israelites from Egypt, recounted in the Bible in the book which bears this name: *Exodus*. The point of departure was the condition of slavery in Egypt, oppression, forced labor. But the Lord has not forgotten his people and his promise: he calls Moses and, with a mighty arm, enables the Israelites to flee from Egypt and guides them through the desert toward the land of liberty.

During this journey from slavery to freedom, the Lord gives the Law to the Israelites, to teach them to love him, the One Lord, and to love each other as brothers. Scripture shows that the exodus is long and tormented: symbolically, it lasts forty years, which is the life span of a generation. A generation which, faced by the trials of the journey, is always tempted to turn back to Egypt. We all know the temptation to turn back. But the Lord remains faithful and those poor people, led by Moses, reach the Promised Land.

This entire journey is carried out in hope: the hope of reaching the Land, and precisely in this sense it is an exodus, an escape from slavery to freedom. These forty days [of Lent] are also for all of us a release from slavery, from sin, to experience freedom, the encounter with the risen Christ.

Each step, each effort, each trial, each failure, and each new start, all have meaning only within the salvific plan of God, who wants for his people life and not death, joy and not pain.

The Paschal Mystery of Jesus is his exodus, by which he has opened the way for us to reach full, eternal, and blessed life. To open this path, this passage, Jesus had to strip himself of his glory, humble himself, be obedient unto death, even unto death on the Cross. Opening the path to eternal life for us cost all his blood, and thanks to him we are saved from the slavery of sin. But this does not mean to say that he has done everything and that we do not have to do anything, that he has passed through the Cross and we "go to heaven in a carriage." It is not like that. Our salvation is surely his gift, but as it is also a love story, he asks for our yes and our participation in his love, as our mother Mary shows us, and after her, all the saints.

This is the dynamic of Lent: Christ precedes us with his exodus, and we cross the desert thanks to him and behind him. He is tempted for us, and has defeated the tempter for us, but we too must face temptations with him and overcome them. He gives us the living water of his Spirit, and it is up to us to draw from his font and drink, in the sacraments, in prayer, in adoration; he is the light which conquers darkness, and we are asked to keep alight the little flame that was entrusted to us on the day of our baptism.

In this sense, Lent is the "sacramental sign of our conversion" (see *Roman Missal*, Oration, Collect, First Sunday of Lent); those who make the Lenten journey are always on the path of conversion. Lent is the sacramental sign of our journey from slavery to freedom, always to be renewed. It is certainly a demanding journey, as it rightly should be, because love is demanding, but it is a journey filled with hope. Indeed, I would add: The Lenten exodus is the journey in which hope itself is formed. The difficulty in crossing the desert—all the trials, temptations, illusions, mirages—all serve to forge a solid, steadfast hope, on the model of that of the Virgin Mary, who, during the darkness of the Passion and death of her Son, continued to believe and to hope in his Resurrection, in the victory of God's love.

With hearts open to this horizon, and feeling that we are part of the holy people of God, let us joyfully begin this journey of hope.

Let us live in the joyful hope of reciprocating to our brothers and sisters, through what little we can, the abundance we receive from God each day.

—POPE FRANCIS

CHAPTER FOURTEEN

Rejoicing in Hope

*W*e know well that the great commandment the Lord Jesus left us is the one about love: to love God with all our heart, with all our soul, and with all our mind, and to love our neighbor as ourselves; namely, we are called to love, to exercise charity. And this is our loftiest vocation, and it is also tied to the joy of Christian hope. One who loves has the joy of hope, of reaching the encounter with the great love that is the Lord.

The apostle Paul, in the letter to the Romans, puts us on guard: there is a risk that our charity may be hypocritical, that our love may be hypocritical. So we must ask: When does this hypocrisy happen? And how can we be certain that our love is sincere, that our charity is authentic? That we are not pretending to do charity or that our love is not for show but a sincere, strong love.

Hypocrisy can insinuate itself anywhere, even in our world of love. This happens when our love is motivated by self-interest and when our service to charity is carried out to draw attention to ourselves or to help us feel good. This is hypocrisy, as when we aspire to things with high visibility, to put our intelligence or our abilities on display for others to see. This is a false, misleading idea, as though charity were a manmade creation, a product of our heart. Charity, instead, is first and foremost a grace, a gift; being able to love is a gift of God, and we must ask for it. He gives it freely, if we ask for it. Charity is a grace: it does not consist in showing off but in what the Lord gives us, which we freely receive, and it cannot be extended to others if it is not first generated by the encounter with the meek and merciful face of Jesus.

Paul invites us to recognize that we are sinners, and also that our way of loving is marked by sin. At the same time, however, one becomes the bearer of a new message, a message of hope: the Lord opens before us a new path of freedom, a path of salvation. It is the opportunity for us, too, to live the great commandment of love, to become instruments of God's charity. And this happens when we let our hearts be healed and renewed by the risen Christ. The risen Lord who lives among us, who lives with us, is capable of healing our hearts: He does so, if we ask it. It is he who allows us, even in our littleness and poverty, to experience the Father's compassion and to celebrate the wonders of his love. And thus we understand that all we can live and do for our brothers and sisters is but the response to what God has done and continues to do for us. Rather, it is God himself, abiding in our heart and our life, who continues to be close and to serve all those whom we encounter each day on our journey, beginning with the least, and the neediest, and in whom he is first recognized.

With these words, rather than reproach us, the apostle Paul wants to encourage us and rekindle hope in us. Indeed, everyone has the experience of not living the commandment of love fully or as we should. But this, too, is a grace, because it makes us understand that we are incapable of truly loving by ourselves: we need the Lord constantly to renew this gift in our heart, through the experience of his infinite mercy. Then, indeed, we will return to appreciating small things, simple, ordinary things.

We will be capable of loving others as God loves them. We will be glad of the opportunity to make ourselves close to those who are poor and humble, as Jesus does with each one of us when we are distant from him, to stoop to the feet of our brothers and sisters, as he, the Good Samaritan, does with each of us, with his compassion and his forgiveness.

The apostle Paul reminds us of the secret of rejoicing in hope. Because we know that in all circumstances, even the most adverse, and also through our own failures, God's love never fails us. Therefore, with his grace and his fidelity dwelling and abiding in our hearts, let us live in the joyful hope of reciprocating to our brothers and sisters, through what little we can, the abundance we receive from God each day.

Finally, in our continuing journey of Christian hope, may we reflect on two words used by Saint Paul: *steadfastness* and *encouragement*. Paul says that both are contained in the message of the Scriptures, but even more, that ours is a God of steadfastness and encouragement. In the Christian life, we are called to spread hope by supporting and encouraging one another. May we always live in harmony with one another, in accord with Christ Jesus, and may we do so with the strength provided by the Lord, who is our unfailing source of hope, always and forever.

Sources

Chapter One: The Comfort of Hope
General Audience, December 7, 2016 (www.vatican.va)

Chapter Two: Reasons for Hope
General Audience, December 14, 2016 (www.vatican.va)

Chapter Three: Hope Is a Journey
General Audience, December 21, 2016 (www.vatican.va)

Chapter Four: Hoping against Hope
General Audience, December 28, 2016 (www.vatican.va)

Chapter Five: Tears of Hope
General Audience, January 4, 2017 (www.vatican.va)

Chapter Six: The Reality of Hope
General Audience, January 11, 2017 (www.vatican.va)

Chapter Seven: Prayer and Hope
General Audience, January 18, 2017 (www.vatican.va)

Chapter Eight: The Language of Hope
General Audience, January 25, 2017 (www.vatican.va)

**Chapter Nine: Christian Hope Is the Expectation of Something
Already Fulfilled**
General Audience, February 1, 2017 (www.vatican.va)

Chapter Ten: The Holy Spirit Is the Living Sign of God's Hope
General Audience, February 8, 2017 (www.vatican.va)

Chapter Eleven: Christian Hope Is Steadfast
General Audience, February 15, 2017 (www.vatican.va)

Chapter Twelve: The Breath of Our Hope
General Audience, February 22, 2017 (www.vatican.va)

Chapter Thirteen: Lent, a Time of Hope
General Audience, March 1, 2017 (www.vatican.va)

Chapter Fourteen: Rejoicing in Hope
General Audience, March 15, 2017 (www.vatican.va)